QUINTA MAZATLAN
A VISUAL JOURNEY

PINO SHAH
EILEEN MATTEI

pino

world heritage photographer
@ artbypino.com +1 956 492 7140

ISBN

Hardcover   9780997998498
Paperback 9780997998412
eBook   9780997998405
IS-02-02-2021

© 2021 by Publisher,
Deval 'Pino' Shah
ArtByPino.com
1007 W US Highway 83
Pharr, Texas 78577
pino@artbypino.com
(956) 492-7140

TYPOGRAPHY, LAYOUT, AND GRAPHIC DESIGN

Carrie Rood
Pino Shah

SPECIAL THANKS

To Erren Seale for the gift of the Folk Art Room logo to this book project and designing the two-page layout. Erren is also the designer of the room and the display cabinets showcasing Arne Moore's collection of 1,400 items.

Mazatlan is a Nahuatl word
describing a place with deer.
Undoubtedly, deer roamed the
native thorn scrub forest here prior
to the settlement of McAllen.

The Talavera tiles do not
misspell the name. In Latin,
the V was pronounced as a U.

Cover - The front pebbled patio, lush with birds of paradise and banana trees, is enclosed by a balustrade that Mexican stone mason Luis de la Garza and an apprentice carved for the Schultzes. The pair also crafted pillars, hearths and other ornamentation over the course of several years.

The Casa de Azulejos (tiles) in Mexico reportedly influenced Jason and Marcia Matthews' design of Quinta Mazatlan. The twelve-foot long Roman tub and walls of blue and white Talavera tile whisper luxury and relaxation. The cantera stone was added by the Schultzes.

A MANSION WITH A MISSION

THE CITY OF MCALLEN ACQUIRED QUINTA MAZATLAN IN 1998 AND IN 2006 OPENED IT TO THE PUBLIC AS A MANSION WITH A MISSION, A WORLD BIRDING CENTER, AND AN URBAN WILDLIFE REFUGE.

Renaissance man Jason Matthews (1887-1964) was extraordinary, and so is the house he and his adventurous wife Marcia built on McAllen's highest elevation and named Quinta Mazatlan.

As an explorer, a freedom fighter for indigenous people, a pioneer in aviation, scriptwriter, composer and storyteller, Matthews traveled the globe. He considered McAllen the 'Crossroads of the Western Hemisphere' and settled there. Influenced by journeys in Mexico, he designed and built Quinta Mazatlan in the late 1930s using more than 10,000 oversize adobe bricks, made on site of local material.

Inside the opulent Spanish Colonial Revival mansion, wide arches framed in hand-painted Talavera tiles combine with Saltillo tile floors and dark beams to create grand, romantic rooms.

Here Matthews conducted hydroponics research, assisted military bands during World War II and, as a patriotic anti-communist, published the politically conservative The (NEW) American Mercury magazine which his wife edited.

Frank Schultz, known as the Grapefruit King, and his wife Marilyn purchased the abandoned mansion in 1968 and restored and enhanced it. In 1987 through their efforts, Quinta Mazatlan received a historical marker recognizing it as among the largest adobe homes in Texas.

The half-circle, second floor space above the kitchen was possibly used as a study originally but the Schultzes used it as a family room.

By linking nature's beauty and cultural history with environmentally sound practices, Quinta Mazatlan demonstrates what we gain by understanding and protecting native habitat and the border heritage. Outside, visitors slow down to smell huisache blooms, listen to Chachalacas chattering, watch butterflies nectaring and touch sandpapery anacua leaves. Inside, elements of good design and materials offer a different kind of tranquility and beauty.

Hidden by lush, semi-tropical gardens and woods, Quinta Mazatlan is an architectural and cultural jewel that has found new life as the Mansion with a Mission. The urban sanctuary connects visitors to local history and the beauty of the natural world.

A version of the Schultz coat of arms, this plaque reflects pride in German heritage and ancestral positions as magistrates.

This original gas lamp welcomed visitors to Quinta Mazatlan more than 70 years ago.

Swiss-born woodcarver Peter Mansbendel, who sculpted the doors at San Antonio's Spanish Governor's Place, carved the mansion's front door. The two laughing gods were modeled on Jason Matthews, complete with goatee. The cherubs below represent Matthews' stepchildren, Edward and Marcia Savage.

The doors' scallop shells, a symbol of travelers in Europe, also signify Columbus' three ships. The Schultzes added the cantera stone frame. Mexican cantera stone is formed of ancient volcanic ash that combined with cirt and shells and over time were compressed in to soft rock. The porous stone is easily carved.

Seventy feet long and twenty feet wide, the elegant Grand Hall showcases the hacienda's signature Saltillo tiles, exposed wooden beams wide arches framed by blue and white Talavera tiles and walls of oversize adobe brick made on site. On the right before the first arch is the original front door. The Schultzes installed the three chandeliers.

Two gas-burning fireplaces warmed the Grand Hall. The carved pecan mantle with the signature scallop shell, the valances and the cantera stone surround were installed during the Schultz era.

Invisible behind fireplace screens, heaters fueled by free natural gas warmed Quinta Mazatlan.

Brass National Electric outlet embedded in the floor

A medieval warrior, archer with bow and arrow and heraldic symbols of a dragon and a rampant unicorn are painted onto leaded glass, a technique dating to the 16th century.

The appearance of paw prints in air-dried Saltillo tiles is supposed to bring good luck.

During renovations, the Schultzes made their marks in wet cement. Karen Schultz was the daughter and Stephen the son.

In-floor safe in the former bedroom closet which was preserved by the City upon renovation.

In the Grand Hall, this tile mosaic replicates the seal of the Royal and Loyal City of Zacatecas, known for its silver mines and its role during the Mexican Revolution. The Schultzes added the chandeliers and the grilles in the tile-framed openings to Cedar Hall.

Elaborately carved furniture reflects the craftsmanship of an earlier era.

The dining room, at one time Frank Schultz' study, was lined with pecan bookcases. The Virgin of Guadalupe tile mosaic indicates the Jason and Marcia Matthews' empathy with the Mexican culture.

Crafted by Santa Rosa artisan Don Gustafson, this carved bookcase now displays a collection of Talavera plates.

Quinta Mazatlan's gift shop was the mansion's original kitchen.

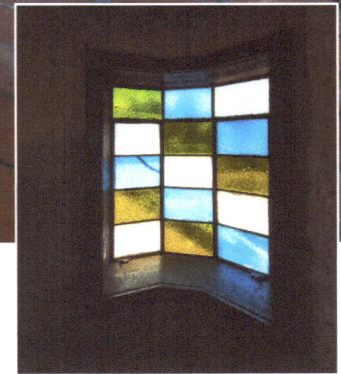

Stairs winding up to the half-circle study above the gift shop are illuminated by faux colored glass windows.

After the Schultzes bought Quinta Mazatlan in 1968, they began restoration and enlarged the mansion to 10,000 square feet. Saltillo tile floors and Talavera tile accents continued in the new garage and storage area, which today serve as offices, a reception area and a video viewing corner.

Commissioned by the City of McAllen after it purchased Quinta Mazatlan, the tile mosaic celebrates the Green Jay, the official city bird. Can you spot the QM?

Quinta Mazatlan's chimneys provide backdrops for custom tile mosaics from Puebla, Mexico. The windows flanking the chimney hold small stained glass panels. The city enclosed this space for a solarium after purchasing Quinta Mazatlan.

Cedar Hall is named for the cedar roof beams, reportedly a gift from the King of Lebanon for Matthews' service during World War I. The wide passageway offers three seating areas, a piano and a shell-shaped fireplace.

Jason Matthews was a composer-lyricist. Marilyn Schultz, who had a music degree, kept pianos and organs throughout her home. She played a piano similar to this rococo 1870s instrument.

Dutch doors into the Grand Hall offer a glimpse of the main fireplace.

Today's low-ceilinged gallery was the master bedroom. The oversize adobe bricks used to construct the mansion are clearly visible here. The City of McAllen replaced the Schultzes' sliding door with the current one. The fireplace retains the original gas fittings.

Off the master bedroom, La Placita, added by the Schultzes, offered a private refuge of palms and flowers.

Marcia Matthews chiseled signs of the Zodiac into the flagstones that formed the front walkway. The Schultzes relocated them to form a patio outside the master bedroom.

The Nahuatl word Mazatlan means a place where deer are found, which explains the numerous deer mosaics at the mansion. Mountainous Puebla has been the center of Talavera production since colonial times.

Flora and fauna are popular tile themes. The mosaic uses Pionono tiles (with yellow right angles) to frame the central palm tile. The possum, a trickster in Mexican folklore, graces a tile at a courtyard gate. The Uriarte logo marks this tile of a turkey posed in front of an oxcart in a frame of Andalulcian-style tile.

Quinta Mazatlan's Talavera tiles come from the Uriarte Talavera workshop in Puebla. Established in 1824, Uriarte is Mexico's oldest producer of Talavera and one of the few certified for continuing the traditional production of tiles with a milk-white glaze, hand painted designs in signature blue, yellow, green, and orange. The glossy tiles have a raised, almost pebbly surface.

Wrought iron grilles outside the Talavera tiles of the kitchen windows added a layer of security.

Displayed outside the Puebla Room, the cockfight mosaic vibrates with life using only five traditional Talavera colors.

Uriarte's Mexican Folk Art series depicts scenes of daily life. Las Quekas is the name given to the tile with the tortilla maker. The Uriarte hallmark is visible in the lower right corners.

Talavera's traditional blue and white tiles with yellow accents feature primarily geometric and floral motifs. Some styles reflect the influence of Arabic and Mediterranean cultures while others echo designs of fifteenth century Spain.

THE FOLK ART ROOM

A COLLECTION THROUGH THE EYES OF ANN Maddox MOORE

And life goes on in villages, with bands playing on the plaza in front of the church to celebrate holidays, holy days and harvests. Folk artists, who often learn their skills as apprentices, excel at capturing moments in the life of their community as well as the bringing to life old tales of strange and magical creatures.

Eye-popping folk art in paper, ceramics, wood, metals, and textiles results from the blending of pre-Hispanic traditions with European cultures and techniques. The willowy, well-dressed skeleton Catrina, sugar skulls, and skeletons (calaveras) at Last Suppers characterize the Mexican view of death as something to joke about and be comfortable with, since it is unavoidable. The dead return on Dia de Los Muertos to eat the food and smell the flowers left by those who remember them.

Recurring motifs in Mexican Folk Art include The Tree of Life, music, the Virgin of Guadalupe, the Day of the Dead and frogs and lizards acting like humans.

The Folk Art Room's eye-popping collection of 1,400 magical, mythical and religious objects and figurines from Mexico flood the senses with color and craft. Ann Moore donated her collection of wood, clay, paper and tin folk art, which is displayed in the former bedroom of the Schultzes' son.

The well at Quinta Mazatlan was used to fill the swimming pool and provide water for the house. The Schultzes planted Washingtonia palms in the courtyard.

Once 12 feet deep and 55 feet long, the swimming pool was built -- before the house -- of the same adobe blocks. Matthews could fill the pool, now much shallower and smaller, in under 30 minutes from the cottage well.

The cottage was Jason and Marcia Matthews' starter home, where they lived while the main house was being built, brick by sun-dried brick. Today, the cottage holds a classroom, meeting rooms, a library and a caterer's kitchen.

Doves are carved into two terra-cotta tiles above the courtyard serving area.

The deer tile mosaic and Talavera tiles and pottery marking the cottage's entrance display a high standard of workmanship. The traditional exposed beams provide support to the heavy roof tile. Natural gas fueled the porch light.

The cottage, which Jason and Marcia Matthews built before the main house, experimented with many architectural and design elements. The Saltillo floor tiles, wooden vigas to support the terra-cotta tile roof and wide arches framed with tiles were all copied in the Main House. Under the left table are samples of the oversize adobe bricks made on site in the 1930s and sun-dried for 30 days. Weighing 70 pounds each, the large bricks provided good insulation in both hot and cold weather.

Native vegetation - prickly pears and agaves - reclaims a concrete irrigation channel that moved water to the citrus groves and fields nearby.

A dry patch of ground provides habitat for three species of cactus.

When the Schultzes added more than 3,000 square feet to the mansion, they echoed existing exterior elements such as roof tiles and adobe walls. Cantera pillars were their own embellishment.

Iron gates on exterior doors and the patio entrances made Quinta Mazatlan a mini-fortress on a hill. The rise marked a natural gas dome that supplied the mansion with free natural gas for 50 years.

Ruby Pond, named for one of Quinta's generous donors, provides habitat for frogs, insects and a bronze great Blue Heron.

On the Forest Trail, this Texas horned lizard sculpture and dozens of other bronzes alert visitors to the wildlife that thrives in the border region. Doug Clark's sculptures of Mexican free-tailed bats, owls, deer, a javelina family and more blend into the landscape.

A LEED Silver building, the Discovery Center combines a science lab with natural history displays and experiential learning areas. The LEED certification means the center is environmentally efficient in design, construction and operation and so uses minimal water and energy.

Inside the Discovery Center, exhibits spark questions and conversations about nature and habitats.

Wide trails wind past thickets of night-blooming cactus to shady patches created by thorn scrub trees such as anacua, with its sandpapery-leaves, husiaches and mesquites.

Performers at the Quinta Mazatlan amphitheater include resident Chachalacas, Green Jays and Kiskadees as well as humans speaking about migrating Hummingbirds and nesting Green Parakeets.

The thorn scrub habitat naturally provides berries, seeds and insects for many different birds, but feeders like these supplement their diet.

Architect Robert Simpson, Quinta Mazatlan's 2014 Conservation Hero, helped design Ebony Grove's four acre habitat, with palapas and benches for wildlife viewing.

Gray Hawk

Gulf Fritillary or Passion Butterfly

Grackle

Long-Tailed Skipper

Zebra Heliconian butterfly

Gray Cracker Butterfly

NOTES

www.ingramcontent.com/pod-product-compliance
Lightning Source LLC
Chambersburg PA
CBHW061153030426
42336CB00002B/28